I0113258

WORDS

UNLEASHED

Publish, Market and Sell
Books Professionally

VMH

VMH Publishing and Books
3355 Lenox Rd.NE Ste 750 Atlanta, GA 30326
www.vmhpublishing.com

Copyright © 2019 by Vikki Jones

All rights reserved.

This book may not be reproduced in whole or in part, in
any form or by means, electronic or mechanical, including
photocopying, recording, or by any information storage and
retrieval system now known or hereafter invented, without
permission from the publisher.

Bulk Ordering Information:

Quantity sales. Special discounts are available on quantity
purchases by corporations, associations, and others. For
details, contact the publisher at the address above or via
email at: info@vmhpublishing.com

Book Cover Design: VMH Publishing
Cover Image: Shutterstock
Interior Layout: VMH Publishing

Hardback ISBN: 978-1-9479-2886-2

Designed in United States of America
Printed in China

10 9 8 7 6 5 4 3 2 1

For all the independent writers in the world.

"

The first moveable type
printing press was invented in
China by an alchemist named Bi Sheng
around the year 1040a.d.
This was an important technological
breakthrough because for the first time
it became possible to
mass produce a text or book incredibly
quickly and efficiently compared
to anything else before. There are still
a few surviving books produced
from the clay-baked moveable type
characters in 12th century China.

Doveton Press

Why Write?

Have you ever considered writing a book? Based on reports and studies, most people feel they "have a book in them". I believe this to be true. Think about it, everyone has a story to tell or something they want to talk about. As a writer and a publisher, I have lots to say on the subject. There is nothing I enjoy more than helping others publish their "voice" through their books. With that said, I want to share six good reasons why you should write your book:

Enlightenment: Believe it or not, writing about certain topics can be incredibly eye-opening. Just as readers travel through a book, learning new things about themselves or the world around them, writers take themselves on a journey of enlightenment as well.

Healing: Depending on the topic a writer chooses to explore, writing can be quite soothing and therapeutic, often offering opportunities to heal from past traumas or anxieties.

Revenue: Many authors are famous and make plenty of money from their books. Granted, the number of wealthy authors may be few, but selling your book is another way to bring in some additional income.

Increased Speakers Fee: If you are already making some or all of your living through public speaking, you may be able to increase your fee if you become a published author. Naturally, the book's content has to run along the same lines as the speech, but a good number of speakers increase their fee simply because they are published authors.

New Ventures: Books have the potential to open doors to other ventures. I've seen a number of individuals (including myself) that started out with a new book that then evolved into an entire business or alternative venture. Had it not been for the book, the new venture never would have crossed their minds.

Getting Your Message Out: If there's something you'd like folks to know, feel or understand, a book is an excellent way to detail your message and say all that you have to say - without time restraints.

On a practical level, whether you are writing books or stories or novels, creative ideas open doors. I've seen a number of folks in today's tech era who have successfully used books as a vehicle to complement or enhance their business ideas, products and services. Books carry a new level of credibility to one's work, particularly when the story is told in a way that captivates readers.

In short writing has a number of benefits, certainly too many to detail here. From my perspective, one of the saddest things in life is when someone leaves their story untold - so if you're in a position to share your story, your ideas, your vision, your dream, do yourself a favor and do it.

To put it succinctly, writing a book:

1. Ignites Passion
2. Educates and Teaches Others
3. Expresses Thoughts Without Interruption
4. Boosts Business Credibility
5. Brings Attention To Your Business
6. Spreads Your Message
7. Generates Revenue
8. Allows You to Market and Brand

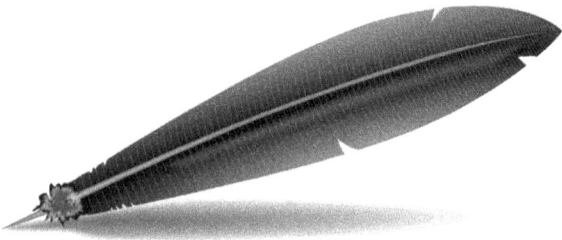

"

Write while the heat is in you.

The writer who postpones

the recording of his thoughts

uses an iron which has cooled

to burn a hole with."

Henry David Thoreau

"

There is no greater agony
than bearing an
untold story inside you.

Maya Angelou

Getting Started

When you start writing, let the words flow. Do not concern yourself with editing. It is okay if words are misspelled and sentences are incomplete. Let out the thoughts that are in your mind, the feelings that are in your heart, and get them on to the paper or computer screen. Stopping to correct the spelling of every word will interfere with the writing process, and inhibit your progress every time.

Editors have a job to do. It is to correct grammar, spelling, punctuation, and diction that writers use. It's the editor's job to ensure that the overall manuscript is comprehensive, and adheres to the language in which it is written. Of course, there are exceptions, such as when writers are trying to maintain certain dialects.

When I wrote my first book, I made it a point to have the discipline, and commitment, to write 5 - 10 pages each night after work. Rain, sleet or snow, I sat at a 'typewriter' and said what I had to say, on paper, each day. For the first few days, it took extra effort to stick to this plan, but after three to four days of doing this, I began to look forward to getting home from work to write my 10 pages. On the weekends, my primary 'to do' was to write 25 pages on Saturday and 25 pages on Sunday.

After three months, I had an almost 1,000 - page manuscript. The key was when I learned to stop interrupting my own writing (editing as I wrote). I determined the number of pages I wanted to write each day, cleared my mind of all other thoughts, and completed my manuscript.

It's important that you clear your mind, so that your thoughts can flow. Clearing your mind is a simple exercise of sitting somewhere in the quiet for a few moments - or however long it takes. That quiet place does not have to necessarily be 'by the sea': it can be a busy coffee shop, or on your terrace. And if you're in a position where you can't leave or find a silent moment, create one: with a pair of noise-cancelling headphones with mellow music, or from an app that plays ocean sounds.

The point is that if you write what comes from within yourself - out of your heart - your feeling will be felt by your readers. Whether you make them laugh, cry, smile, gain knowledge, or guide them through a process, they will embrace the energy of your read.

Now pick up that pen, get on that keyboard, or if you don't want to do either of those, pick up a recorder and start talking. Let those thoughts flow, and do not interfere with your writing by correcting misspellings and run-on sentences! Leave that to the editor!

A Few Quick Writing Tips:

1. When you write, let it come from the heart. Readers will connect with what you've written if it is authentic.
2. Create a detailed outline for each subjects you wish to share (talk about). If it's a novel, imagine your characters, write their profiles, create your plot and the scenes.
3. Do not concern yourself with misspellings, punctuation, or syntax. This is what editors are for.
4. Determine a quiet writing location, block off a period of time to write, and allow

no interruptions. This includes phones, streaming devices, talking with others, etc. If necessary determine an exact amount of pages you'd like to complete each time you sit down to write. Ex.: Monday - Thursday after dinner five pages each evening; Saturday 20 pages, etc.

5. While you write, focus on your words, not your marketing plan. Determining your target audience and other details can be done after your creative work is complete.

6. Open your mind and express yourself as you would with a friend or neighbor.

7. Remember your job as a writer is to write, nothing more. The team that publishes your manuscript will polish the work and manage the other details.

If I had not had the opportunity to write and publish my own book, I would not be where I am today. Your book will take you places, but if you're doing it for fame and money only, these material things generally won't last. Whatever you choose to do, do it for the right reasons and make wise choices.

"

The Gutenberg Bible is the
first great book printed in
Western Europe from movable metal type.
It is therefore a monument that
marks a turning point in the art of
bookmaking and consequently
in the transition from the
Middle Ages to the modern world.
The printing of the Bible
was probably completed late
in 1455 at Mainz, Germany.

Library of Congress

"

A word is dead

When it is said,

Some say.

I say it just begins

to live that day.

Emily Dickinson

Understanding Book Publishing In The Digital Era

You have a wonderful story, but publishers and book retailers are in this business to make money. They're looking for a polished, marketable product. So what do you do if your following is small and you have little sales guarantee? Let's address a few critical areas of publishing and marketing that are important for your work.

Traditional Publishing or Self-Publishing

There is a great deal of confusion about the differences between self-publishing and traditional publishing. You might be asking yourself, "What do these words mean?" or

"What do I do?" Well, before choosing a form of book publishing, you can do your research to ensure that you are going where you feel your book belongs.

Self-publishing means one thing: you're doing it yourself. You gather what you've written, you click and upload the text yourself, and design your own book cover to present to the literary market. As you might expect, there are a few problems when it comes to self-publishing. One of them is the quality of the work. If the book is poor quality or if it's not associated with a reputable or established publisher, the book is probably not reaching its full potential. The other problem is whether major stores will accept "click and upload" work into their stores. You need to understand that bookstores, whether online or brick and mortar, are a business. Granted, there are some local, independent bookstores that are supportive of new self-published authors, and really want to help get their work out there, but those people also have bills to pay. They need to know that somebody is willing to buy the book being placed in their store. A bookstore is still a business.

Traditional publishers are those who will pay for your manuscript. They may give authors an advance payment because the book will sell on the backend of the publication's business, and the company will then get their money through royalties. Oftentimes, writers are looking to get paid for their manuscript. If you want to submit your work to a traditional publisher, you should be mindful of how you plan to sell it. Sometimes you have to go through a literary agent, and other times you may bypass the literary agent and land an offer yourself, but the point is that you still have to sell your work.

Having a strong following prior to publishing also helps because companies, even traditional publishers, are in business to make money. They don't want 5,000 books sitting on shelves gathering dust with no one to buy them. It is helpful to have a platform, whether through social media, website, television or radio, from which you can advertise your book to your own followers. You may need to have numerous followers before traditional publishers even decide to look at your manuscript, and even then, the book itself must be well written.

This is not to discourage or dissuade you, nor is it to have you feel that success is unlikely. In order to succeed in this industry, you must understand the difference between self-publishing and traditional publishing, as well as non-traditional publishers - which is where we at VMH fit in.

At VMH, the author is given more control than she might have with the traditional publishing model. However, there are some limits when it comes to design, manufacturing and distribution. Our books have mainstream appeal with mainstream publishing components. The books are distributed in a global centralized database so that if a bookstore wants to stock your book, you have a better chance of getting it on the shelves. We also don't take any of your work's royalties. We work on our portion of the marketing and ensure that your book has been properly polished and that it's marketable and ready to compete with books from other mainstream publishers.

The rest is up to you. You still need to do your part by marketing your book. Marketing to your own followers is free publicity, and even people who are known internationally, those who are already wealthy or famous, still have to put in the work.

Books are items that people have to purchase just as they would music from YouTube or iTunes. For this reason, as an author, you should hold book tours as if you were a musician or artist. The publicist or PR representative designates various cities and states for the author to visit to meet fans and promote their book. If you hope to be a successful and recognized author, then you have to work hard to get your book out there.

Making Money Selling Your Book - Signing at a Bookstore

When you begin writing a book with the intention of publishing, the main idea is to ensure you will have readers. How do you do that? One strategy is to get books into the hands of consumers through bookstores or online retailers. A bookstore allows consumers to venture in and browse through shelves filled with books of all topics. When people go into a bookstore, however, most folks already have a book in mind, unless of course they're just browsing.

The reality is that if you're an author and you have been given the space to showcase your book, you need to capitalize on the opportunity by letting customers know you're there. Don't be afraid to engage with people because, believe it or not, they want to know what you're doing and what you're passionate about. Engagement with potential readers is key to a successful outcome.

As a book publisher, I've worked with many independent authors who became a success. No, they were not famous people, but these independent authors created a space for themselves and engaged their immediate audience. They made appearances on the front page of newspapers, on radio shows, mainstream televised shows, and in various magazines. As a result, they're making sales while enjoying their work. You can be happy too. Buckle down on a strategy, do your research, and invest. Don't pursue the cheap route. If you don't have the money, you will have to find a way to keep within your budget, but still publish with the best possible quality.

When you are granted book signings, be sure to engage directly with shoppers. You're there to interact with new people. Don't be shy. Talk to them.

Marketing Plan, Partnering & Book Sells

A compelling story is nothing without a dynamic marketing plan. Former First Lady Michelle Obama's book *Becoming* has surpassed any other book deal requested of presidents in history. Despite her fame before publishing her autobiography, the success of her book is not solely attributed to her status as a former First Lady.

Michelle Obama's book was so successful in part thanks to a number of partnerships, social media, and televised media. Social media platforms are useful for all authors, not just those who do not have celebrity friends like Valerie Jarrett, Oprah, and Sarah Jessica

Parker like Michelle Obama. Social media gives authors access to friends of friends as well as websites that make suggestions based off of individuals' searches and likes. Michelle Obama's book is honest and authentic when discussing personal subjects that people don't know about and may not discuss. As powerful as her story is, this book would not have been nearly as successful without her marketing strategies.

It takes a strong marketing plan with many of the components that I just named in order for your story to sell well and widely. Creating a strong marketing plan for yourself will also open doors to speaking engagements and other business opportunities. A good marketing plan is vital for any sort of success and any potential revenue.

Advertising Is Not Solely About the Sale

Advertisers advertise to sell their products. The idea is to attract new customers, but oftentimes there is also another concern in advertising: branding. Both are essential to successful marketing.

When advertisers place ads and get their message out there through advertising, it's not solely about the sale. Granted, it would be phenomenal if every time an advertisement is placed, sales come in, but the goal of the ad is not just to create a sale through advertising, but also to expand one's customer base.

Remember: people don't purchase because you're forcing them to do so. They have the freedom to spend their money however they choose. You need to make people know you're there, you have a product or a service that may interest them or can meet a need that they did not know they had.

I Need to Sell More of My Books! How?

What is it that attracts new customers to a business? How do you reach the people that you're looking to reach effectively within your budget? I found one of the things that matters most is your online presence. They say to never judge a book by its cover, but as a species we are drawn to the attractiveness of a product. It may sound shallow, but the reality is when you compare the two, studies have shown that when something looks aesthetically pleasing it is more likely to sell. As consumers, we are drawn to items that look good even if we are spending a little more.

As a seller, how can you make your product look fantastic and stand out from the rest? One way is by starting with high quality photography or videography to advertise your book; low resolution will not cut it. Authors that are self-publishing or working with a non-traditional publisher need to ensure that the book cover is attractive in order to compete with books from traditional publishers.

There is nothing wrong with creating your own book cover, especially if you have budget restraints. But if you have the means, pay for professional quality artwork. This applies to any type of product to draw the eye of brick and mortar stores. All businesses, including mainstream, independent, and small shops care about how things appear on their shelves. Buyers walk into stores and are immediately drawn to attractive items. For example, I went into a store and saw three similar types of dark chocolate popcorn. Even though the popcorn was packaged in the same way, I purchased the slightly more expensive popcorn because of its unique branding and design. I knew I was ultimately paying for the packaging, but I was attracted to the style and branding of this product in particular.

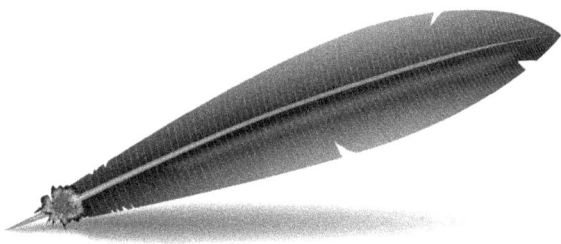

"

Get it down.

Take chances.

It may be bad, but it's the

only way you can

do anything really good.

William Faulkner

Book Publishing is a Business

Book publishing, like any other industry in the world, is a business. It all boils down to sales. The politics of it is whether the product that you have, your book, is going to sell. That is where the conversation begins and ends. For most major retailers, most book publishers, major literary agents, and those with book to film adaption in the industry, you have to ask yourself whether your product is well made and marketable enough for sales.

The reality is that book publishers who pay advances or take on a manuscript project are placing a bet that it's going to sell; they make this assumption because generally those authors already have a major following either through social media, television, or other means, which equates to sales. Generally, popularity leads to sales because on a fundamental level, the world buys a product because someone popular says it's great.

With that said, you should think of this when it comes to your book in retail. If your primary motivation is, "I want to be on Amazon and Barnes and Noble," and so forth, you need to ask yourself a question. Can you pull in thousands, if not millions, of dollars with what you have to say? What I'm going to share with you now is how you and the manuscript you've written can find success without compromising the integrity of the work or your creativity.

This book is not for those who write quick books. This is for the people who've written something that they're passionate about and want to spread to the widest possible market. You may be a famous person reading this book with a great deal of social capital in hand already - if so, why not bet on yourself against the big publishers? They're putting their money on you because they know you can sell. Why not sell it yourself? Cut out the middleman.

You might feel that you do not have enough time to allocate towards publishing a book, and that's fine too - but there are still ways to remove the middleman and publish without interrupting your life. Traditional publishing is based on a system that has been disrupted, exposed, and is trying to maintain a gate-keeping mentality in the 21st century. Those that are already rich and famous have the power to cut out the middleman.

Should I Write or Hire a Ghostwriter?

Let's imagine that you have a story to tell or information that you'd like to share with readers, but you're not necessarily sure how to begin writing. Perhaps your schedule does not even allow the time it takes to write a book. How do you get started? How do you go about writing a book when you don't have time to write or you may not know where to begin? This is not a new problem, and the solution is a popular one. This is where ghostwriters come in.

For those who have very busy schedules or are sticklers about their time, ghostwriting has long been a solution to this question. Ghostwriting is the process of someone else writing your story for you.

In order for a ghostwriter to take on this task, they have to study the subject that you want to discuss, or interview you extensively in order to have the necessary background to write your book. Ghostwriting is a solution for a number of high-profile individuals.

What does ghostwriting entail? How much does it cost for those that are busy executives or celebrities? Generally, the cost is not a question. Instead, the concern is how long it might take. A ghostwriter is defined as a person who writes your story, but they do not get the credit for it unless there's an agreement between the writer and the actual author. The ghostwriter is like a ghost in that they aren't there beyond the words on the page.

Quite frankly, ghostwriters often totally disappear after the job is done (depending on the agreement between the ghostwriter and the author). They may receive credit on the copyright page or they may just remain silent and not get any credit at all. Whether the author of the book is the true writer of the actual book, the copyright generally goes to the author, not the ghostwriter. That means their name will not go in the book. The actual book itself will be credited and named the author. Although it may seem unconventional, this process is really just a contract like any other. The ghostwriter is paid an upfront fee that's negotiated between him and the storyteller.

Ordinarily the ghostwriter ensures that their final product meets the standards set by the contract: i.e., the book is completed number of pages, edited professionally, and ready for book publishing. This is common in ghostwriting. Many celebrities, politicians and executives don't write their own stories because of scheduling and the time it takes to sit down and write a book. Even though you have a very tight schedule, it is important that you allocate however many hours to the project that you have agreed upon in your conversations with the ghostwriter.

My company has written books for those who simply couldn't put the pen to the paper or fingers to the keyboard. Generally, a ghostwriter hired because they are skilled conversationalists. I refer to dialogues between the author and ghostwriter as *conversations,* although some may refer to them as interviews. The point is the ghostwriter connects with the author in order to write the story the author wishes to tell. The ghostwriter needs to have good communication skills and must be able to establish trust with the individual that they're working with. The individual should want to open up and share their knowledge of the subject they want written about, so making sure he or she is comfortable is key.

It's important for the ghostwriter to ask questions and fact check certain subjects to ensure that there's clarity for the reader and accuracy to the original story. Generally, there's a first draft and then they go back through for a second draft. If there's a story being written that includes real life experiences, even if it's a business book, it's only natural that the storyteller might forget a detail here or there. So, there may be a first draft of a book or a manuscript in its entirety, and when the author reads it, he or she will remember something else. As things begin to come to mind, the ghostwriter should have the ability to pull the story out of the author so that this new story is seamlessly integrated into the rest of the book.

The ghostwriter also has the responsibility of ensuring that the manuscript flows in a way that readers can digest. As stated previously, ghostwriters are generally used for high profile individuals who simply don't have the time to write or for those who don't know where to start. There are also writing coaches available for those who would like to write their own stories but don't know how to begin. If they do know where to start, they may just not be able to get it out. Ghostwriters assist with accurate translating the author's story or subject matter to the page in time for the publishing process to begin.

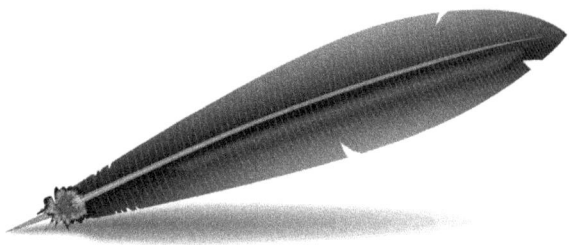

Amazon

Amazon is one of the most popular online book retail sellers in the world. It has been deemed the "largest store on earth" and has millions of products, including books. When a general consumer is looking to buy a book, they tend to go to Amazon first. Therefore, Amazon is the best place for your book if you are an independent author.

An independent author is someone who has not signed with a book publisher or been paid in advance for their manuscript. Amazon is the largest online bookstore in the world. This places Amazon in a position to sell a vast area of books across disciplines and subjects.

When it comes to products that are listed and advertised on their website, Amazon has total control. If any of you have a website right now, you know that you can add things to your website, and you can take things away from your website as you please. The same is true of Amazon. Amazon can take things off their website, add things to their website, change the prices of certain items, or not show images of products at any time.

When an author has a new book out on the market, that book is distributed, meaning it is sent through a centralized American publishing system that goes out globally. This system allows for books to be made available for purchase or stock at libraries, various bookstores, Walmart, Barnes and Noble, or your school.

Generally, when writers do not use Amazon's direct publishing platform, it seems algorithms toy with information surrounding the sale of their books. Information that might be affected by these changes includes: pricing, shipping time, stock availability, and at times the book's image. With that said, there are many ways that you could approach publishing and distributing your book. You simply have to make the best choice for you.

Your book may be listed with 15 other books appealing to the same market. You have to make the decision as to whether or not you want to self-publish with Jeff Bezos' platform which is only designed for Amazon, or if you want to use a centralized system that distributes your book to all these other platforms, or if you want to do it all yourself by designing your own website and brand. If people *truly* want your book, they will choose to come to your website and buy it.

Website

Here's the simplest way to sell your book in the disrupted book retailing industry: build a website and sell your book. If you don't want to build a website, you still need a storefront. You don't need Amazon to sell your product. You also don't need big names in the retail book industry to endorse you or your writing in order to sell your book. They will just take a cut of the profits anyway. Remember, *you* are the reason that the book is selling, and you don't need those big names or middlemen.

So why don't you sell your book yourself? Build your website, list your book on your website, and include an introduction and some information about yourself. If it's a business book, make your objectives known. If it's a cookbook, put a sample recipe on there. For a children's book, you could go so far as to share the moral of the story or a little bit about the main character. Building a website does not cost much. You have a lot of web tools like Wix and Squarespace where you can actually build sites to sell products. So why not create your own store? That cuts out the need for places like Barnes and Noble and Amazon.

Depending on the kind of book that you have, you could sell it both independently and through a seller like Barnes and Noble. My suggestion is to maintain your independence by ensuring that you have your books in bulk when it's time for author signings or speaking engagements. Some of us are accustomed to certain brands and we think, "I want my book in this store". There's nothing wrong with that. But remember that retailers are getting a percentage of your profit. There's not necessarily anything wrong with them taking a cut, so long as you remember that there are alternate ways of approaching the publishing process. Do your research on retail space, but just remember that you can easily sell your book by yourself with a simple website.

"

If we encounter
a man of rare intellect,
we should ask him
what book he reads.

Ralph Waldo Emerson

Manuscript Submission

As an independent author seeking to publish your book without a literary agent or a successful submission to one of the "Big Five", you still have to go through a literary agent to get your manuscript out there. When submitting, it is required that you submit a polished, complete manuscript. "Polished" does not necessarily mean proofreading to excess, but rather ensuring that whatever has been written is complete. Once your work is submitted, the book publishing process begins, so it's important that you have a clean, polished manuscript ready to go. Whether you're working with an independent publisher or a mainstream publisher, preparation is essential to success. Ensure that you've said all that you need to say in every paragraph. You'll know when you're done.

Sales and Marketing

Whatever it is that compelled you to read this book. I encourage you to carry that sense of purpose with you as you write and market your own book.

Passion is a driving force. Passion causes people to move when nothing else around them is moving. Purpose and passion are intertwined and mandatory components of any successful project. If you don't have the passion for your work, or if you've lost your passion for your work, you need to find a way to regain each or pursue a new project which lends you that same joy. Purpose and passion are important for anything that you're doing, including the book that you've written and have yet to publish.

If you write with purpose and passion, you can create something that can open people's minds and help them learn something new.

You could also encourage unity within communities and bring about change. Every kind of book, whether it's for children, a cookbook, memoir, or a business books all have power to bring about change. And I hope whatever you've written and are ready to put out into the world will inspire readers just as the story inspired you to write.

Selling Your Book to Your Immediate Audience

Selling your book offers the next greatest feeling after your book has been professionally published, distributed, and made available to readers. Now that the written work is done, how do you plan to place your book in the hands of readers? This is the question that should be answered next - or at least considered. Your book is ready to go. You may have completed all phases or already distributed. The next most important thing that you can do is ensure that folks are seeing and becoming interested in your work as a result of marketing, publicity, and media.

Your objective is to get your book into the hands of readers and ensure they feel well informed or entertained by what you have written. There are many ways that you can go about that. The first step that you can take is reaching out to your followers, especially those who are already directly in front of you. Reaching out to people that don't know you as soon as your book hits the market or as you're beginning the preorder phase of your book is an excellent next step. I've seen the success of so many writers who successfully market their work starting with those that are already around them.

If you own a business, people who are familiar with your work would be your first readers or people of interest. Of course, you can always expand this network domestically or globally. But don't forget about the people that are in front of you when it comes to boosting your sales and readership. If you have events, it's important to stage events around you that are accessible to both you and your followers. For instance, if there is a conference, your book is a business book, and you've been brought on as a speaker, be sure that you have your book available there for purchase immediately after you finish with your segment. If you deliver a great speech, people are sure to want more from you. Be prepared and have your books there and be ready to take their payments. You can take payments through a number of different forms, including cash or apps run through mobile devices.

The other component of this process that you can consider is publicity and the media, which can include television shows, talk shows, and social media. Videos are a great way to get people to see you. They listen to what you as an individual have to say. It prompts them to want to know more about you and your work, so they are then inspired to buy your book from your website or another retailer.

This book has presented you with various ways for you to be able to publish professionally and make your book available to people. Now you have a responsibility to get out there and tell people you have a book that you're excited to share with them – and it's available for purchase.

You can also consider hiring a publicist or PR firms. Hiring a publicist is a critical component for those who have the budget to do so. A publicist is someone who can get you out there, get your message out, and direct traffic to your book through an already established network of connections. Advertising is another way to share the message about your book. There are a number of other ways for you to spread the word about your book. Family, friends, and other folks around you are supporters who want to cheer you on and help you boost your sales. Your topic is of interest to them, so keep that in mind.

You also have to let people know that you have a story to share that is available to them for purchase. This is where your marketing and strategy comes in handy. Don't think listing on Amazon or Barnes and Noble will automatically make people buy your book.

There are millions of books out there. What will make yours stand out to readers?

Publish Yourself Professionally

Let's boil it down.

If you're interested in professional publishing, here are the steps you will need to follow:

1. Complete manuscript in its entirety, polished (to the best of your ability) and ready to go.
2. Send manuscript to copyright office.
3. Determine the style of book publishing that best suits your need.
4. Contact the publishing company either directly or via a literary agent.
5. The book publishing process begins!

If you're on a low budget or without a book publisher, here are the steps you'll follow:

1. Hire a reputable editor.
2. Hire a reputable book cover designer that's familiar with dimensions - this is necessary to ensure the book cover design is compatible with book printers.
3. Hire a typesetter or a professional book layout designer.
4. Purchase an isbn number and bar code from bowker.
5. Create an account with Ingramspark and/or kdp (for those that require simpler tech use).
6. Load files to your Ingramspark and/or KDP account.
7. Hire a graphic artist to create promotional designs for social media and advertisements. (Companies like fiverr are very budget friendly).
8. Create social media pages and/or a website promoting your new book.
9. Hire a publicist or contact press directly to share your new book with the new world.
10. Set a release date.
11. Print on demand or print in bulk.

Traditional Publishing Note
(doing the math)

"If a publisher prints 5,000 copies of a book at $3 per unit and sells it at retail for $12, it seems like the publisher will earn a large margin: $15,000 in printing costs versus $60,000 earned at retail. But if that publisher only sells 500 copies because the book is by a relatively unknown, debut author, they are already in the hole for $9,000. And that doesn't take into account the retailer's cut of the profits, the cost of distribution, the cost of storing books in a warehouse, not to mention other overhead costs." - Book Business Mag.

"

Great books

help you understand,

and they help you

feel understood.

John Green

Sales, Mindset Recap

Driving Traffic to Your Personal Brand Instead of Amazon

Amazon is the largest online book retailer in the world, but at the end of the day, it's better for your book and your brand if people purchase directly from your store..

If you are a business owner, realtor, speaker, or athlete and have written a book, you may feel that the best way to go when 'selling' your book is to list it in retail stores. There's nothing wrong with that instinct, particularly because the average customer buys many of their products from that platform. But if a person truly wants to purchase your book or any other product, they will buy it from anywhere it's sold - including your website.

Why not drive traffic up by referring people to your website when asked where your book can be purchased? When folks go to your website, they can learn more about you and what you have to offer. In seeking out your book, customers will be introduced to your brand, ultimately expanding your work and reach.

Here's what I need you to know. If you have a product to sell, I need you to think outside of the box and understand that you have the capacity to expand your reach far beyond the simplest route for selling books quickly. That system is not for everyone, especially for those publishing cookbooks.

Generally, cookbooks require a unique style of book printing. Quality images of the dishes attract customers and amplify the mouth-watering appeal of your food. Choosing the wrong printing and distribution system will greatly diminish the impact of the food stylist and food photographer's work. Some printers do not offer gloss or semi-gloss paper for printing books and if they do, the cost of the quality paper will force you to increase the price of your cookbook. To boil it down, there are three major factors that you need to figure into your consideration of the cost breakdown and expected profits from your book:

1. Print cost of each book
2. Shipping cost of each book
3. Marketing cost for the book

These three factors are essential to consider - when you print each book at a high cost and sell with a retailer who takes a cut of the profit, how much income will you actually gain?

In order for a product to sell, it has to first capture consumer attention and then meet the standard at which it was advertised. If you know that you have created a quality product, vitality is critical that you focus on elevating its public appeal. Any images or artwork on the cover or inside the book require high-quality paper, printing, and a book cover design that will stand out from the rest. With all these components in place, my advice is not to send people to a third-party retailer to purchase your book. Instead, you can direct your fans to come buy it directly from you... your website.

If you already have a following, whether large or small, tell people to come check out your website and all that you have to offer. This is a guaranteed way for them to learn more about your business, restaurant, other products, and you as a person and author. Your brand will grow; people will remember you and your website just as they remember Amazon when they think of a book.

"

Writings are your voice,
it's what you want to say
to the world
or the place you want to
create for the world.
Make good choices for
'distributing' your voice.

Vikki Jones

"

To ensure a spot on
The Wall Street Journal's
Bestseller list,
you need to sell about
3000 books in the first week
and to hit gold and the
New York Times Bestseller list,
you'll need 9,000 copies sold
in the first week.

Book Promotion Hub

Best Seller Lists & Book Marketing

"I want my book to make a Best Seller list – Amazon Best Seller, New York Times Best Seller, any bestseller list that has national or international focus."

There's no harm in having that goal, but what is your action plan to achieve it? What does that plan really look like? How do you get **your** book to the top?

Marketing, promoting, and any other means of spreading the word about your book are the keys to getting your book to the top of that list. At the heart of your marketing efforts should be the desire to tell people about your books and compel them to buy a copy. Marketing comes in many forms, including:

- print advertisements
- having others publicly endorse your book
- radio interviews
- vlog and blog interviews
- television appearances
- social media

Your local news and radio stations is a great start that may get you comfortable with getting the word out there. Internet radio shows with a large number of listeners in your target audience are also an excellent outlet for self-promotion. Not all outlets are created equal, and the costs of each will vary. If you know someone with connections to national media outlets, this would be a great time to call in a favor with them. There is no such thing as a plug & play or one-size-fits all marketing strategy. You have the freedom to choose any media outlet in which you find the most comfort within your budget.

Social media is a great organic platform for marketing your book. Start with your inner circle and encourage them to help you get the word out. Start a Facebook, Instagram, YouTube, Google+, or Twitter page for your book and share it widely. If you already have a sizeable social media following, you can promote your book through your existing accounts. Share a few excerpts from your book. Organize public readings and book signing events to meet your followers and attract new followers. Search your posts for loyal fans who consistently share, mention, or "like" your online content, and reach out to them about spreading the word. Seek out YouTubers and vloggers who share content that aligns with the principles or themes in your book. Offer to send them a complimentary copy to review in exchange for a message to their community.

Your book may not make the best seller list instantaneously –promoting it across multiple platforms will take effort and time. Partnering with a notable publisher and experienced publicist can certainly help you accomplish the goal quicker and more easily. The New

York Times best seller list may be a lofty goal, but the Amazon Best Seller list may be more attainable. (To make the New York Times Best Seller list, you must sell roughly 5,000 to 10,000 copies within the first week of your book launch or in any given week.)

No matter what type of product you are promoting – books, shoes, food, services – you still have to let people know it exists and help them understand why they need it. Word by word, platform by platform, interview by interview, you have to appeal directly to the consumer and garner interest in your book. You must connect with your audience and let them know why purchasing your book would be more satisfying than buying another book or spending their valuable money on other items. They will believe in your content if they see that you genuinely believe in it too. Do not shy away from being open with your audience. Your authentic engagement with your followers could be the very thing that converts someone to being a loyal member of your fanbase.

Every audience interaction you have will not result in a guaranteed book sale, which is why it is even more important to use a combination of several different marketing strategies in order to reach as many people as possible. Get your face and your message out there in connection with your book. The more people you can reach, the closer you become to making a best sellers list.

I do hope I've helped you develop an open strategic marketing plan for increasing book sales. I look forward to reading your best-selling works soon.